Read-About® Geography

Living in
the Tundra

By Donna Loughran

Consultant
Nanci R. Vargus, Ed.D.
Assistant Professor of Literacy
University of Indianapolis, Indianapolis, Indiana

Children's Press®
A Division of Scholastic Inc.
New York   Toronto   London   Auckland   Sydney
Mexico City   New Delhi   Hong Kong
Danbury, Connecticut

Designer: Herman Adler Design
Photo Researcher: Caroline Anderson
The photo on the cover shows a Sami boy feeding a reindeer.

Library of Congress Cataloging-in-Publication Data

Loughran, Donna.
  Living in the tundra / by Donna Loughran.
    p. cm. − (Rookie read-about geography)
Summary: Introduces the frozen tundra environment and some of the people
and animals that dwell in tundras.
  ISBN 0-516-22738-6 (lib. bdg.)   0-516-27331-0 (pbk.)
  1. Tundras–Juvenile literature. 2. Natural history–Arctic
regions–Juvenile literature. 3. Indigenous peoples–Arctic
regions–Juvenile literature. [1. Tundras.] I. Title. II. Series.
  QH84.1.L69 2003
  577.5'86–dc21
                                         2003003900

CHILDREN'S PRESS, and ROOKIE READ-ABOUT®,
and associated logos are trademarks and or registered trademarks
of Scholastic Library Publishing. SCHOLASTIC and associated logos
are trademarks and or registered trademarks of Scholastic Inc.
2 3 4 5 6 7 8 9 10 R 12 11 10 09 08 07   62

Brrrrr. Can you feel
the icy wind?

You can, if you live on the tundra (TUHN-druh).

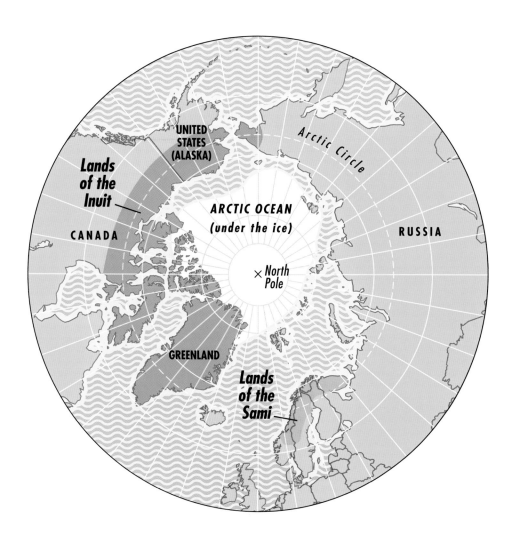

Lands of the Inuit

UNITED STATES (ALASKA)

Arctic Circle

ARCTIC OCEAN
(under the ice)

CANADA

RUSSIA

× North Pole

GREENLAND

Lands of the Sami

This is the tundra. Look around. What do you see?

You can see lots and lots of ice.

It is too cold for trees to grow here. Winter is long. Summer is short.

Musk ox

Arctic hare

Animals like the musk ox
and hare come here to eat.

Arctic tern

In the summer, the snow
and ice melt. Clouds of
insects fly over the land.
Birds come to eat them.

Caribou (KA-ri-boo) come to eat the plants that grow.

Caribou

Tundra swans

Then summer ends.
The birds fly away.

The caribou move south.
The animals look for food
in warmer lands.

Some Inuit (IN-yoo-it) people live on the tundra. They build houses above the ice.

Dogsled

They travel across the ice in snowmobiles (SNOH-moh-beelz) and on dogsleds.

In the winter, Inuit hunters hunt for seals.

The seals swim near the land and rest on the ice.

In the summer, hunters hunt caribou.

The hunters also fish in the cold waters.

Most Sami (SAW-mee) people live and work in cities. Others hunt on the tundra.

Some Sami herd reindeer (RAYN-dihr) on the tundra.

Reindeer are like caribou.

Some people call the Sami the reindeer people.

The Sami people have many different words for reindeer in their language (LANG-gwij).

Most people do not know how to live and work on the tundra. The Inuit and Sami do.

They have lived here for
a very long time. It is
their home.

The tundra is a special place. In the summer, the sun does not set.

In the winter, colorful lights flash across the dark sky.

When would you like to visit the tundra?

Words You Know

caribou

dogsled

reindeer

Sami

tundra

Index

About the Author

Donna Loughran is an artist, writer, and multimedia designer.
She lives in Austin, Texas.

Photo Credits

Photographs © 2003: Corbis Images: 27, 31 top right (Charles & Josette Lenars),
9 (Kennan Ward); Peter Arnold Inc./Kim Heacox: 18; Photo Researchers, NY:
15, 25, 30 bottom (B & C Alexander), 21 (Marcello Bertinetti), cover (Donnezan/
Explorer), 11, 30 top (Michael Giannechini), 17 (Dan Guravich), 26 (Lawrence
Migdale), 12 (Rod Planck); Stone/Getty Images/David Hiser: 3; The Image
Works/Norbert Rosing/UNEP: 28; Visuals Unlimited: 6, 31 bottom (N. Pecnik),
10, 22, 31 top left (Tom Walker); Wolfgang Kaehler: 8, 14.

Map by Bob Italiano